McGraw-Hill Education

ENGLISH
ILLUSTRATED
DICTIONARY

LiveABC

Mc Graw Hill Education

New York Chicago San Francisco Athens London Madrid
Mexico City Milan New Delhi Singapore Sydney Toronto

1 2 3 4 5 6 7 8 9 10   CTP/SGC   1 0 9 8 7 6 5 4

ISBN 978-0-07-183957-0 (book and CD set)
MHID   0-07-183957-7 (book and CD set)

ISBN 978-0-07-183954-9 (book for set)
MHID   0-07-183954-2 (book for set)

Library of Congress Control Number 2014934163

MP3 Disk

The accompanying disk contains MP3 recordings of all terms presented in this dictionary. These files can be loaded onto your MP3 player.

To load MP3 files on your iPod or similar MP3 player:
1. Open iTunes on your computer.
2. Insert the disk into your computer and open via My Computer.
3. Drag the folder "English Dict MP3s" into the Music Library in the iTunes menu.
4. Sync your iPod with iTunes and eject the iPod.
5. Locate the recordings on your iPod by following this path:

    Main menu: Menu
    Music menu: Artists
    Artist menu: English Dictionary: Sections 1–3

                English Dictionary: Sections 4–9

                English Dictionary: Sections 10–15

McGraw-Hill Education products are available at special quantity discounts to use as premiums and sales promotions or for use in corporate training programs. To contact a representative, please visit the Contact Us pages at www.mhprofessional.com.

This book is printed on acid-free paper.

Contents

How to Use This Book

It is suggested that you listen to the audio recordings when using this book. It will make your learning more efficient.

Unit title

Category title

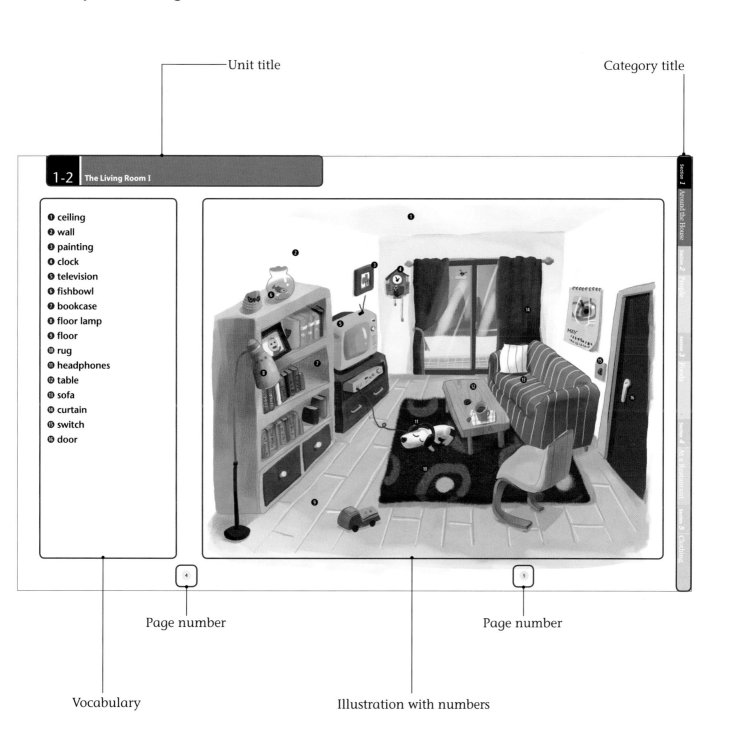

1-2 The Living Room I

Section 1 Around the House
Section 2 People
Section 3 Foods
Section 4 At a Restaurant
Section 5 Clothing

❶ ceiling
❷ wall
❸ painting
❹ clock
❺ television
❻ fishbowl
❼ bookcase
❽ floor lamp
❾ floor
❿ rug
⓫ headphones
⓬ table
⓭ sofa
⓮ curtain
⓯ switch
⓰ door

4

5

Page number

Page number

Vocabulary

Illustration with numbers

1

❶ building
❷ window
❸ swimming pool
❹ main door
❺ doorman
❻ apartment
❼ balcony

❽ top floor

❾ stair

❿ garage

⓫ yard

⓬ mailbox

❶ ceiling

❷ wall

❸ painting

❹ clock

❺ television

❻ fishbowl

❼ bookcase

❽ floor lamp

❾ floor

❿ rug

⓫ headphones

⓬ table

⓭ sofa

⓮ curtain

⓯ switch

⓰ door

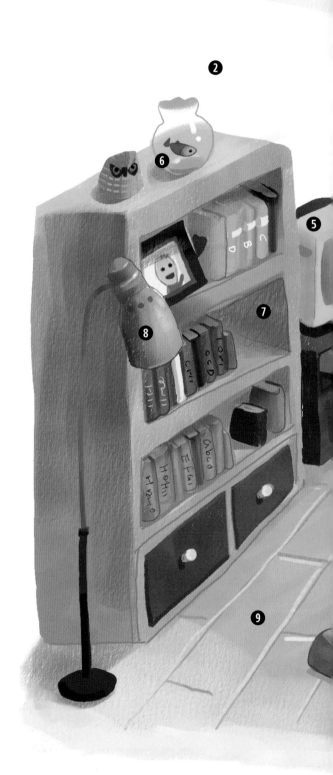

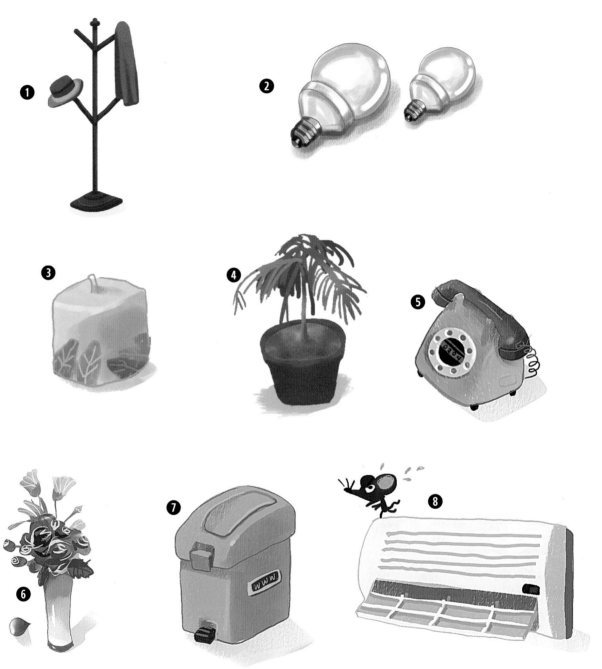

❶ coatrack
❷ light bulb
❸ candle
❹ potted plant

❺ telephone
❻ vase
❼ trash can
❽ air conditioner

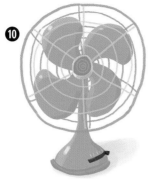

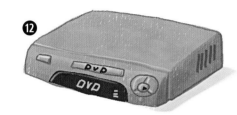

⑨ heater

⑩ fan

⑪ stereo

⑫ DVD player

⑬ remote control

⑭ vacuum cleaner

⑮ answering machine

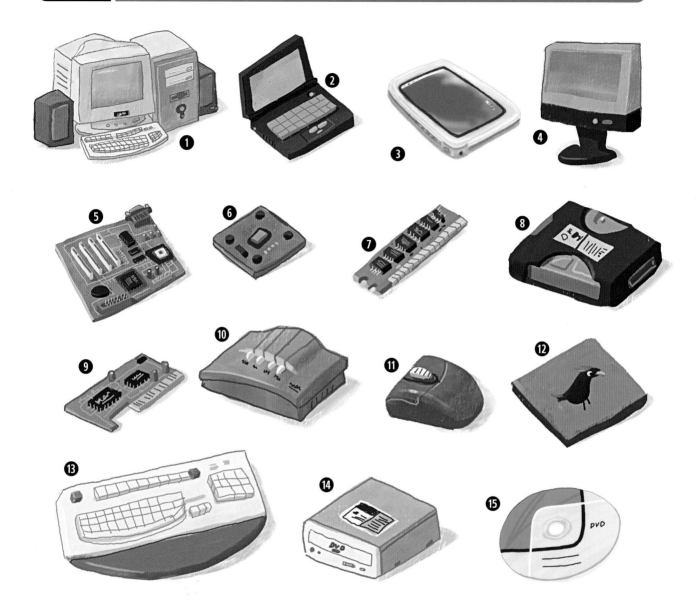

❶ desktop computer

❷ laptop computer

❸ tablet PC

❹ LCD monitor

❺ motherboard

❻ CPU

❼ RAM

❽ hard disk

❾ network adapter card

❿ modem

⓫ mouse

⓬ mouse pad

⑬ keyboard

⑭ DVD-ROM drive

⑮ DVD

⑯ CD burner

⑰ hub

⑱ speaker

⑲ card reader

⑳ flash drive

㉑ scanner

㉒ webcam

㉓ printer

㉔ fax machine

㉕ photocopier

1. tile
2. shelf
3. mirror
4. socket
5. bath towel
6. towel
7. sink
8. faucet
9. toilet paper
10. toilet tank
11. toilet
12. drain
13. bath mat
14. shower curtain
15. showerhead
16. bathtub

1. razor
2. electric razor
3. hand cream
4. facial wash
5. shampoo
6. conditioner
7. shower gel
8. soap
9. body lotion
10. toothbrush
11. toothpaste

⑫ blow-dryer

⑬ hairbrush

⑭ cotton swab

⑮ nail clipper

⑯ facial tissues

⑰ perfume

⑱ scale

⑲ laundry basket

⑳ bathrobe

㉑ shower cap

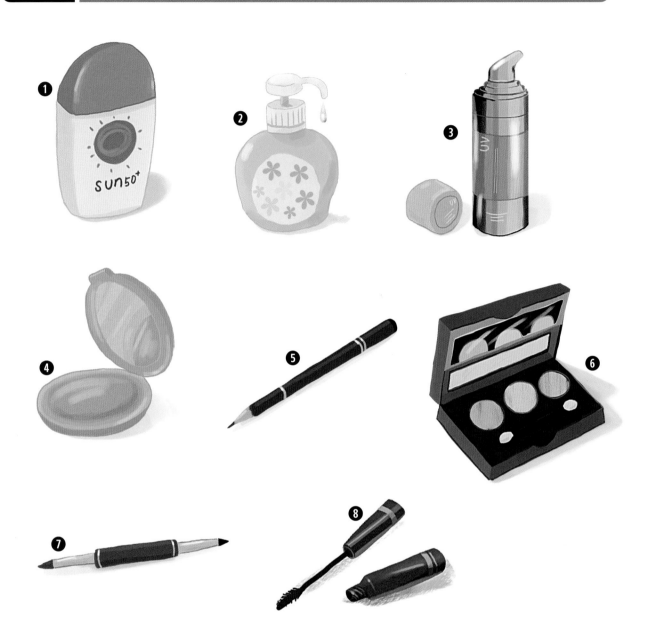

❶ sunscreen

❷ moisturizer

❸ foundation

❹ compact foundation

❺ eyebrow pencil

❻ eye shadow

❼ eyeliner

❽ mascara

❾ eyelash curler

❿ blush

⓫ brush

⓬ lipstick

⓭ nail polish

⓮ cleaning oil

⓯ mask

❶ alarm clock

❷ picture frame

❸ lamp

❹ nightstand

❺ headboard

❻ pillow

❼ double bed

❽ mattress

❾ sheet

❿ comforter, duvet

⓫ slippers

⓬ wool blanket

⓭ footstool

⓮ chest of drawers

⓯ bookend

⓰ wardrobe

⓱ cosmetics

⓲ vanity

Additional Information: Kinds of Beds

1. **single bed**

2. **sofa bed**

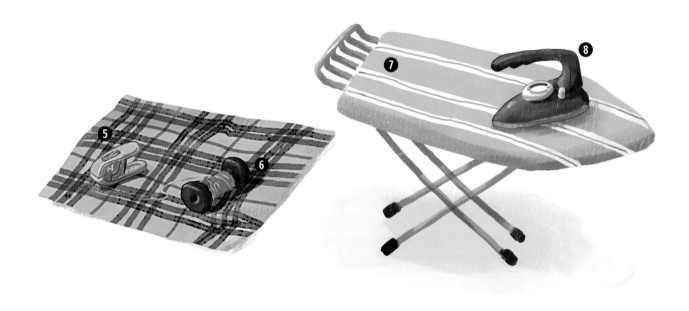

❶ laundry detergent

❷ fabric softener

❸ bleach

❹ hanger

❺ clothespin

❻ thread

❼ ironing board

❽ iron

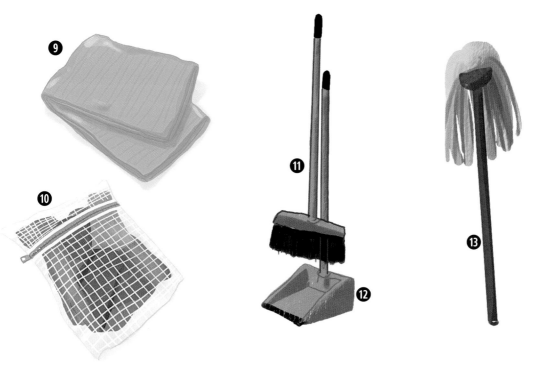

⑨ rag

⑩ laundry bag

⑪ broom

⑫ dustpan

⑬ mop

⑭ washing machine

⑮ dryer

❶ refrigerator

❷ apron

❸ coffeemaker

❹ range fan

❺ cupboard

❻ microwave oven

❼ dishrack

❽ ladle

❾ leaver

❿ frying pan

⓫ gas stove

⓬ wok

⓭ sink

⓮ counter

⓯ cutting board

⓰ dishwasher

⓱ oven

⓲ cabinet

⓳ blender

⓴ steam cooker

㉑ electric thermos pot

㉒ toaster

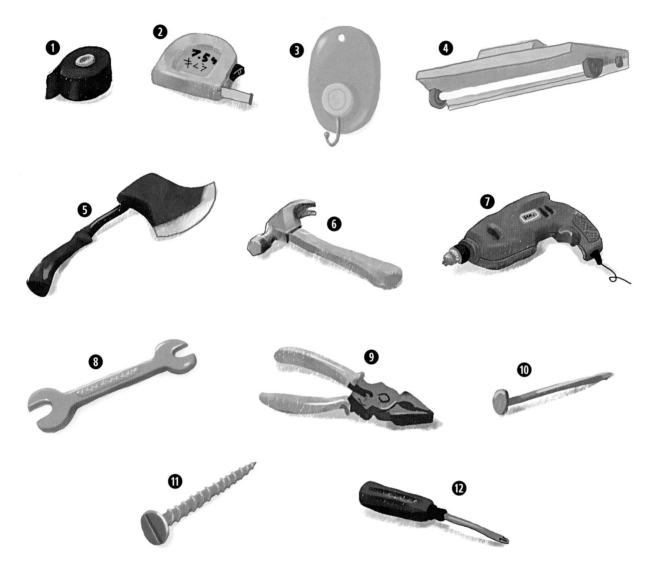

1 tape

2 tape measure

3 hook

4 fluorescent light

5 ax

6 hammer

7 electric drill

8 wrench

9 pliers

10 nail

11 screw

12 screwdriver

⓭ flashlight

⓮ toolbox

⓯ paint

⓰ paintbrush

⓱ paint roller

⓲ ladder

⓳ shovel

⓴ scrub brush

㉑ bucket

㉒ sponge

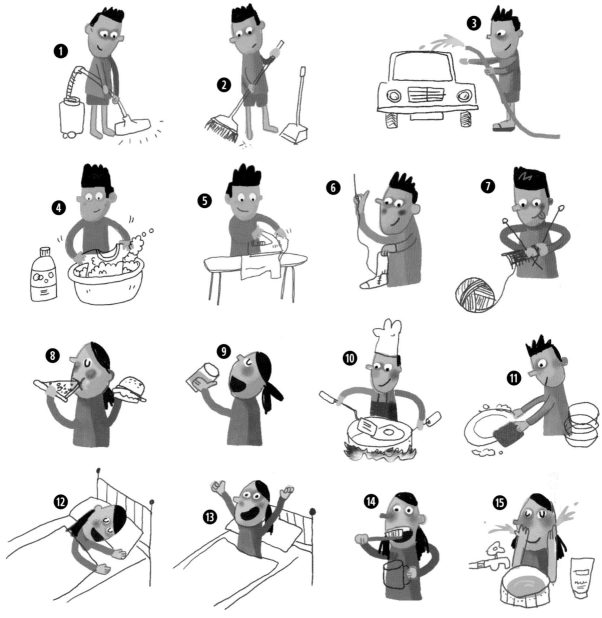

❶ to vacuum

❷ to sweep the floor

❸ to wash

❹ to do the laundry

❺ to iron the clothes

❻ to sew

❼ to knit

❽ to eat

❾ to drink

❿ to cook

⓫ to wash the dishes

⓬ to sleep

⓭ to get up

⓮ to brush one's teeth

⓯ to wash one's face

⓰ to take a shower

⓱ to get dressed

⓲ to wear (accessories)

⓳ to take off

⓴ to call, to telephone

㉑ to water the plants

㉒ to take out the garbage

㉓ to open/ turn on

㉔ to close/ turn off

25

❶ man

❷ woman

❸ elderly man

❹ elderly woman

❺ middle-aged person

❻ boy

❼ girl

❽ teenager

❾ pregnant woman

❿ toddler

⓫ child

⓬ baby

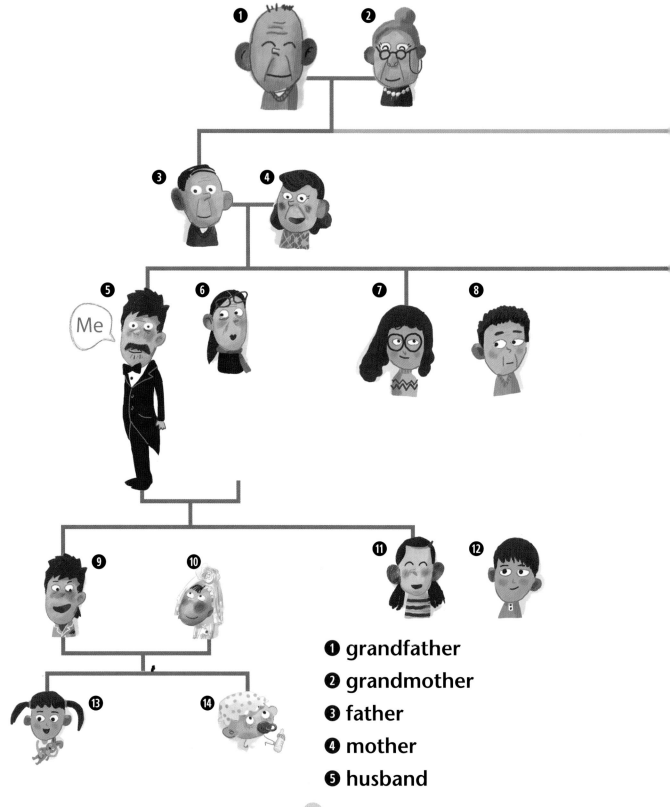

1. grandfather
2. grandmother
3. father
4. mother
5. husband

relatives

 parents

spouse

father-in-law mother-in-law

stepson stepdaughter

children

⑮ aunt

⑯ uncle

⑫ son-in-law

⑬ granddaughter

⑭ grandson

⑮ aunt

⑯ uncle

⑰ brother

⑱ sister-in-law

⑲ cousin (son of aunt and uncle)

⑳ cousin (daughter of aunt and uncle)

㉑ nephew

㉒ niece

❻ wife

❼ sister

❽ brother-in-law

❾ son

❿ daughter-in-law

⓫ daughter

❶ salesman, saleswoman

❷ assistant

❸ secretary

❹ manager

❺ reporter

❻ teacher

❼ professor

❽ civil servant

❾ police officer

❿ firefighter

⓫ soldier

⓬ driver

⓭ pilot

⓮ farmer

⓯ fisherman, fisherwoman

⓰ chef

⓱ architect

⓲ mechanic

⓳ carpenter

⓴ laborer

㉑ plumber

❶ doctor

❷ nurse

❸ scientist

❹ engineer

❺ politician

❻ businessman, businesswoman

❼ entrepreneur

❽ lawyer

❾ judge

❿ tour guide

⓫ broker, agent

⓬ actor

⓭ actress

⓮ singer

⓯ hairstylist

⓰ artist

⓱ musician

⓲ dancer

⓳ sculptor

⓴ athlete

THE INTERNA

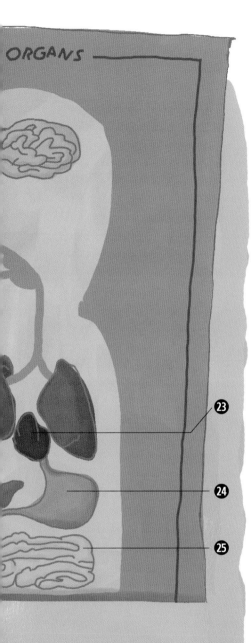

ORGANS

➊ head

➋ eyelash

➌ eye

➍ cheek

➎ neck

➏ waist

➐ hand

➑ foot

➒ hair

➓ forehead

⓫ eyebrow

⓬ nose

⓭ tooth

⓮ mouth

⓯ chin

⓰ chest

⓱ belly

⓲ navel

⓳ thigh

⓴ brain

㉑ lung

㉒ liver

㉓ heart

㉔ stomach

㉕ intestines

❶ happy
❷ excited
❸ relaxed

❹ surprised
❺ angry
❻ embarrassed

 ❼

 ❽

 ❾

 ❿

 ⓫

 ⓬

❼ shy

❽ nervous

❾ to smile

❿ to laugh

⓫ to cry

⓬ sad

❶ to slip

❷ to fall down

❸ to stand

❹ to kneel

❺ to squat

❻ to do a handstand

❼ to walk

❽ to crawl

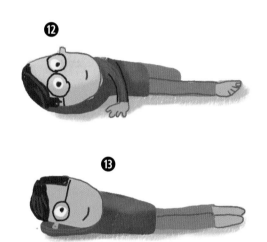

❾ to jump

❿ to kick

⓫ to sit

⓬ to lie down

⓭ to lie facedown

⓮ to carry (something) on (one's) back

⓯ to stretch

❶ turnstile

❷ frozen foods

❸ dairy products

❹ beverages

❺ canned food

❻ packaged food

❼ bread

❽ microwave food

❾ shopping bag

❿ membership card

⓫ free sample

⓬ meat

⓭ seafood

⓮ vegetables

⓯ fruit

⓰ shopping cart

⓱ customer

⓲ basket

⓳ cash register

⓴ scanner

㉑ cashier

㉒ plastic bag

㉓ cash

㉔ receipt

㉕ deli food

CANNED FOODS 5 PACKAGED FOODS 6 BREAD 7 BREAD READY MEALS 8 SNACKS

INFORMATION DESK

DELI FOOD 25

VEGETABLES

1 pineapple
2 plum
3 strawberry
4 cherry
5 melon
6 cantaloupe
7 watermelon
8 papaya
9 mango
10 persimmon
11 pear
12 kiwi fruit
13 lemon
14 passion fruit

⑮ tangerine

⑯ orange

⑰ grapefruit

⑱ grapes

⑲ star fruit

⑳ apple

㉑ banana

㉒ guava

㉓ blueberries

㉔ raspberry

㉕ peach

㉖ apricot

㉗ pomegranate

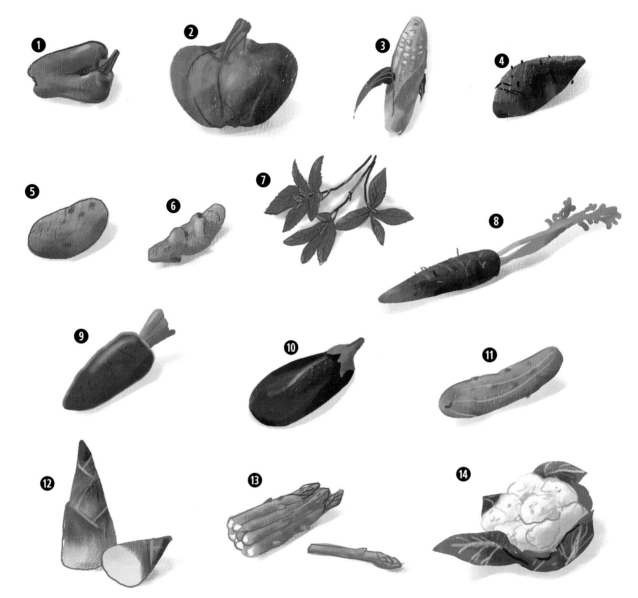

❶ green pepper
❷ pumpkin
❸ corn
❹ sweet potato
❺ potato
❻ ginger
❼ basil

❽ carrot
❾ radish
❿ eggplant
⓫ cucumber
⓬ bamboo shoot
⓭ asparagus
⓮ cauliflower

⑮ cabbage

⑯ lettuce

⑰ bean sprouts

⑱ broccoli

⑲ spinach

⑳ mushroom

㉑ tomato

㉒ celery

㉓ onion

㉔ green onion

㉕ garlic

㉖ brussels sprouts

㉗ red cabbage

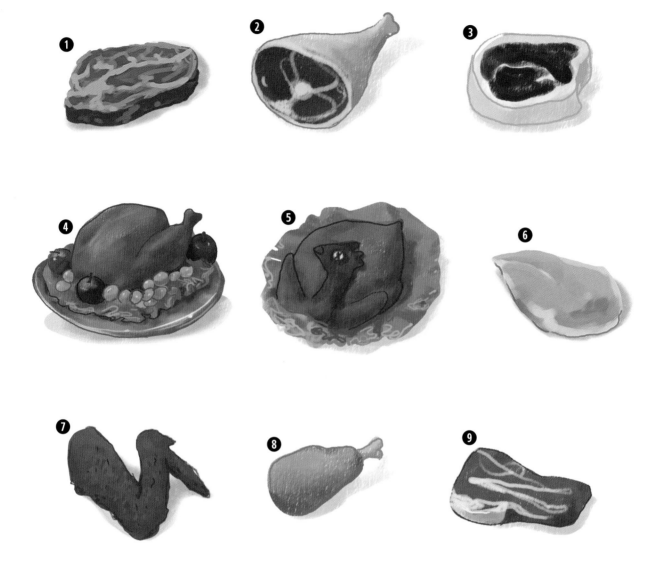

❶ lamb

❷ leg of lamb

❸ beef

❹ turkey

❺ chicken

❻ chicken breast

❼ chicken wing

❽ chicken leg

❾ pork

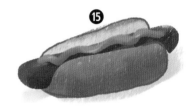

⑩ ground meat

⑪ ribs

⑫ meatballs

⑬ bacon

⑭ ham

⑮ hot dog

⑯ sausage

⑰ salami

⑱ jerky

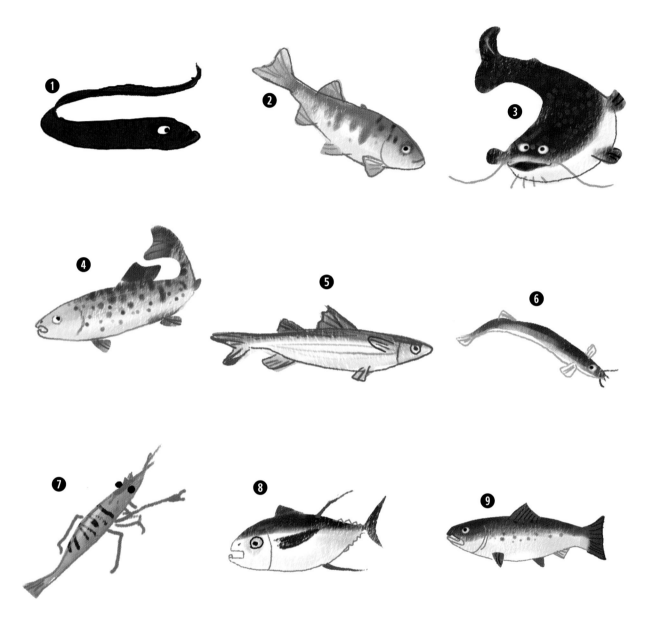

❶ eel

❷ trout

❸ catfish

❹ grouper

❺ gray mullet

❻ loach

❼ shrimp

❽ tuna

❾ salmon

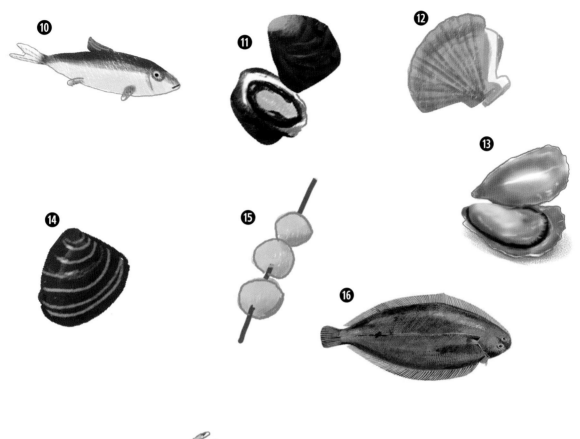

⑩ cod

⑪ abalone

⑫ scallop

⑬ oyster

⑭ clam

⑮ fish ball

⑯ (Dover) sole

⑰ squid

⑱ octopus

❶ cola

❷ soda

❸ smoothie

❹ coffee

❺ hot chocolate

❻ iced tea

❼ mineral water

❽ lemonade

❾ juice

3-7 Dairy Products

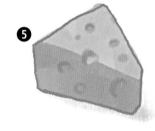

❶ butter
❷ cream
❸ ice cream
❹ frozen treat
❺ cheese
❻ yogurt

❼ drinking yogurt
❽ milk shake
❾ non-fat milk, skim milk
❿ low-fat milk
⓫ whole milk

51

❶ pickles

❷ paper napkins

❸ straw

❹ doggie bag

❺ pancakes

❻ chicken nuggets

❼ doughnuts

❽ onion rings

❾ croissant

❿ to go

⓫ stool

⑫ hamburger

⑬ for here

⑭ french fries

⑮ serving tray

⑯ bagel

⑰ fried chicken

⑱ muffins

⑲ waffle

❶ waiter
❷ ice cube
❸ ice bucket
❹ teapot

❺ coffeepot
❻ waitress
❼ tablecloth
❽ menu

❾ pepper shaker

❿ salt shaker

⓫ bill

⓬ toothpicks

⓭ place mat

⓮ napkin

⓯ hostess

⓰ counter

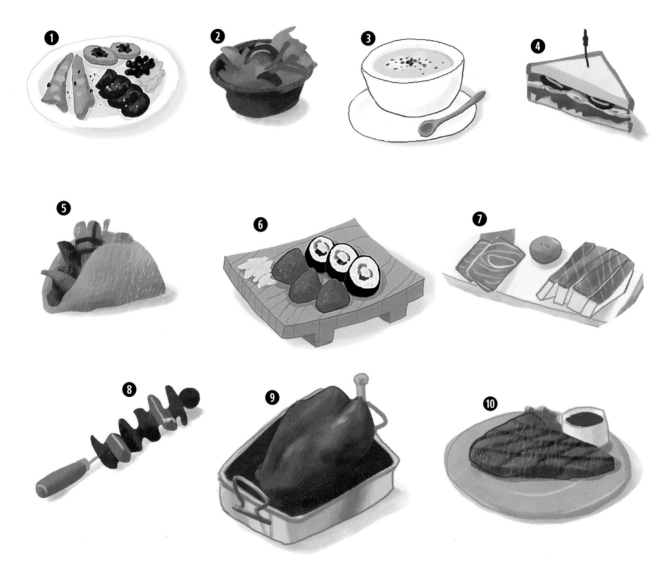

❶ appetizer

❷ salad

❸ soup

❹ sandwich

❺ taco

❻ sushi

❼ sashimi

❽ shish kebab

❾ roast chicken

❿ steak

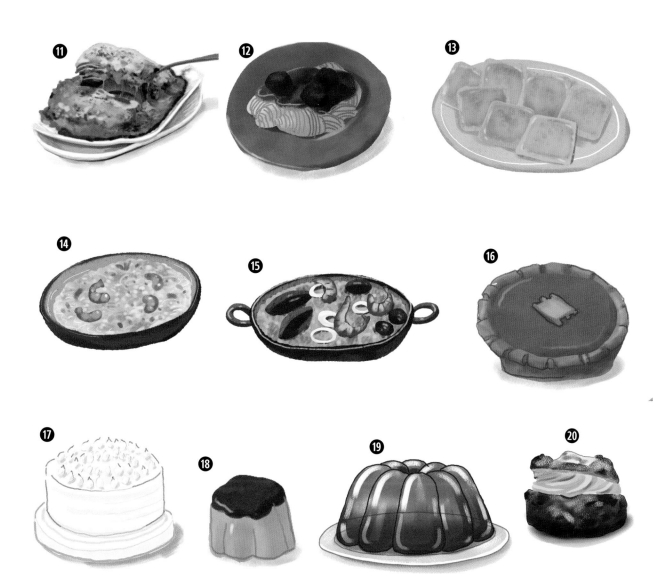

⑪ lasagna

⑫ spaghetti

⑬ ravioli

⑭ risotto

⑮ paella

⑯ apple pie

⑰ cake

⑱ pudding

⑲ gelatin

⑳ cream puff

❶ chopsticks

❷ fork

❸ dessert fork

❹ spoon

❺ teaspoon

❻ salad spoon

❼ steak knife

❽ dinner knife

❾ butter knife

 ⑩

 ⑪

 ⑫

 ⑬

 ⑭

 ⑮

 ⑯

 ⑰

⑩ bowl

⑪ platter

⑫ plate

⑬ soup plate

⑭ saucer

⑮ water glass

⑯ mug

⑰ beverage coaster

1 to bake

2 to grill

3 to barbecue

4 to fry

5 to stir-fry

6 to pan-fry

7 to simmer

8 to boil

9 to blanch

10 to stew

11 to steam

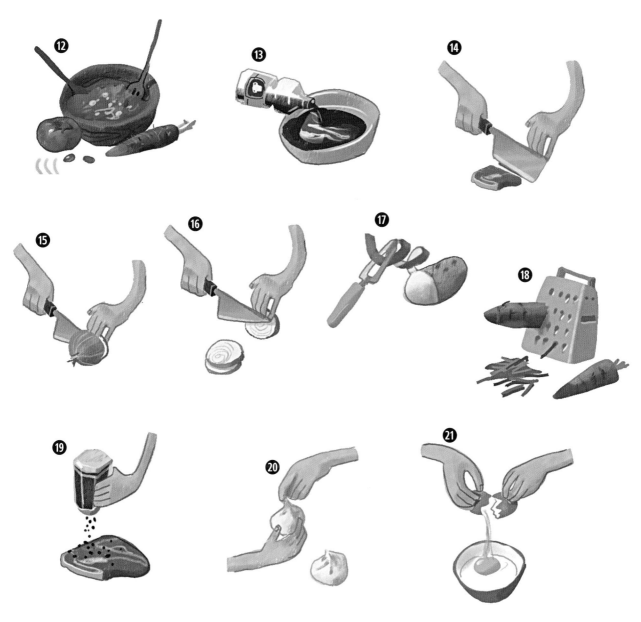

⑫ to toss

⑬ to marinate

⑭ to chop

⑮ to cut

⑯ to slice

⑰ to peel

⑱ to grate

⑲ to sprinkle

⑳ to wrap

㉑ to crack (an egg)

❶ rock sugar

❷ brown sugar

❸ salt

❹ pepper

❺ vinegar

❻ wine

❼ cooking oil

❽ olive oil

❾ soy sauce

❿ sesame oil

⓫ fish sauce

  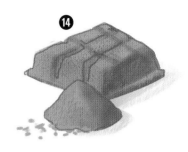

⑫ cornstarch

⑬ potato starch

⑭ curry

⑮ mustard

⑯ ketchup

⑰ wasabi

⑱ chili sauce

⑲ cinnamon

⑳ caviar

5-1 Clothing

❶ dress
❷ gown
❸ suit
❹ shirt
❺ vest

❻ T-shirt
❼ skirt
❽ pants
❾ jeans
❿ shorts

⑪ boxers

⑫ sweater

⑬ jacket

⑭ down coat

⑮ sportswear

⑯ uniform

⑰ raincoat

⑱ pajamas

⑲ bra

⑳ underwear

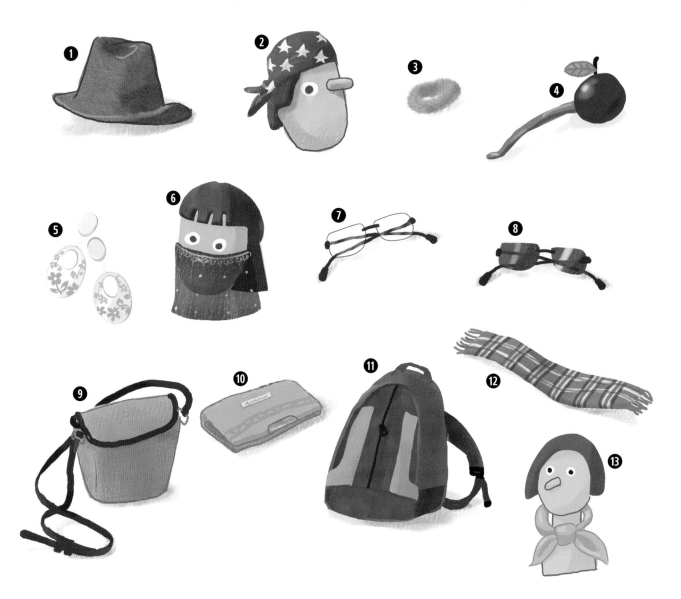

❶ hat

❷ bandana

❸ hair band

❹ hair clip

❺ earrings

❻ veil

❼ eyeglasses

❽ sunglasses

❾ purse

❿ wallet

⓫ backpack

⓬ scarf

⓭ silk scarf

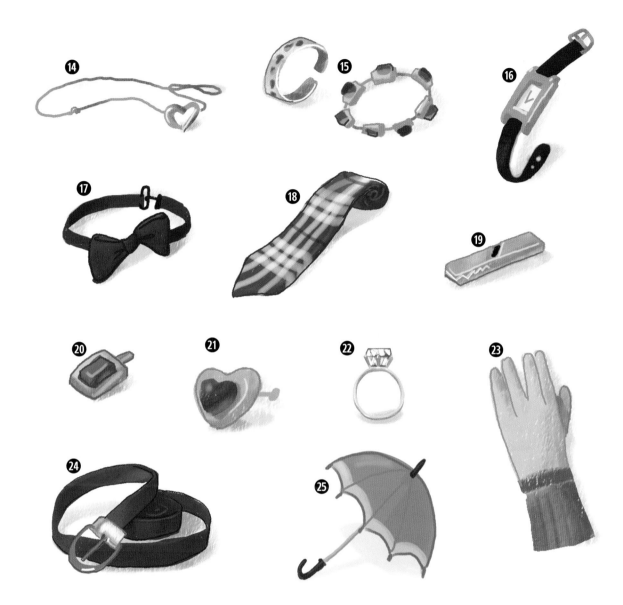

⑭ necklace

⑮ bracelet

⑯ wristwatch

⑰ bow tie

⑱ necktie

⑲ tie clip

⑳ cuff link

㉑ brooch

㉒ ring

㉓ glove

㉔ belt

㉕ umbrella

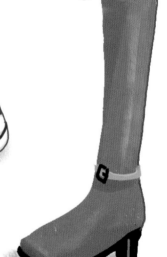

❶ shoes

❷ leather shoes

❸ high heels

❹ pointed shoes

❺ canvas shoes

❻ boots

❼ sneakers

❽ sandals

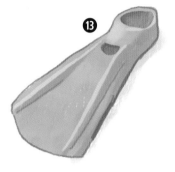

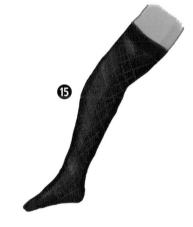

❾ slippers

❿ flip-flops

⓫ rain boots

⓬ snowshoes

⓭ flippers

⓮ socks

⓯ stockings

⓰ panty hose

❶ department store

❷ karaoke club

❸ street

❹ appliance store

❺ convenience store

❻ restaurant

❼ bank

❽ hospital

❾ post office

❿ vending machine

⓫ hotel

⓬ gym

⑬ bookstore

⑭ furniture store

⑮ nightclub

⑯ tea house

⑰ coffee shop

⑱ pharmacy

⑲ movie theater

⑳ police station

㉑ toy store

㉒ bakery

㉓ beauty salon

㉔ delicatessen

❶ letter carrier

❷ mailbox

❸ package

❹ express mail

❺ letter

❻ return address

❼ postmark

❽ envelope

❾ stamp

❿ registered mail

⓫ recipient's address

⓬ zip code

⑬ airmail letter

⑭ ordinary mail

⑮ postcard

⑯ card

⑰ maritime mail

⑱ airmail

⑲ e-mail

⑳ text message

❶ police station
❷ plainclothes officer
❸ traffic officer
❹ police cap
❺ whistle

❻ patch
❼ badge
❽ gun
❾ police baton
❿ handcuffs

⓫ thief

⓬ patrol officer

⓭ police dog

⓮ police motorcycle

⓯ patrol car

⓰ to call the police

⓱ robber

⓲ written report

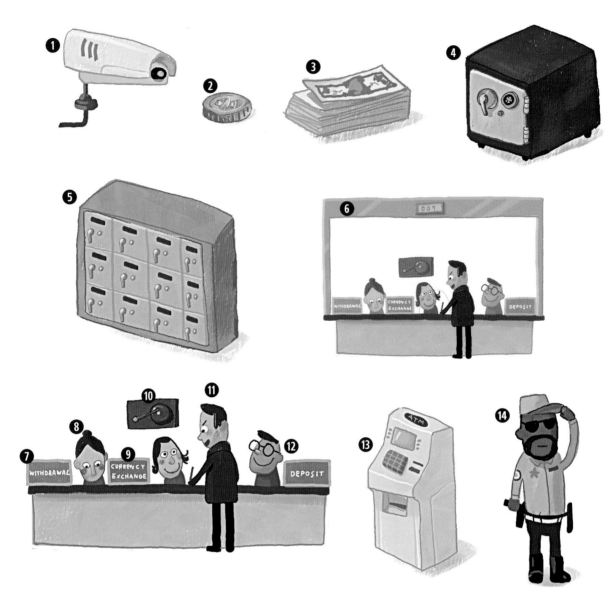

1. security camera
2. coin
3. bill
4. safe
5. safe-deposit box
6. counter, window
7. withdrawal
8. teller
9. currency exchange
10. alarm
11. to open an account
12. deposit
13. ATM
14. security guard

⑮

⑯

⑰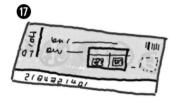

⑱

⑲

⑳

㉑

㉒

㉓

㉔

㉕

USD		33.400	33.940	34.440
JPY		28.440	28.740	29.340
EUR		45.520	45.770	46.620
TWD		0.840	—	1.150

⑮ armored truck

⑯ money order

⑰ check

⑱ traveler's check

⑲ passbook

⑳ ATM card

㉑ credit card

㉒ ID card

㉓ stamp

㉔ signature

㉕ exchange rate

① elevator

② display counter

③ salesclerk

④ women's department

⑤ lingerie department

⑥ lost-and-found department

⑦ escalator

⑧ household appliances department

⑨ furnishing department

⑩ teen department

⑪ sporting-goods department

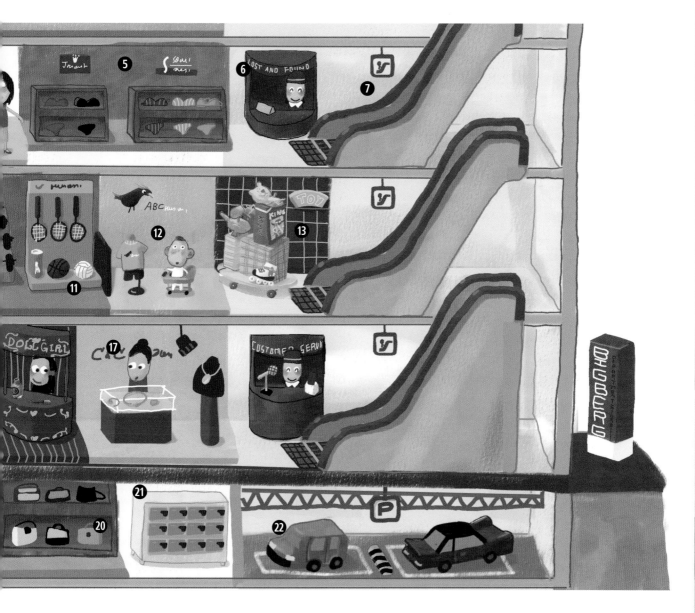

⓬ children's department
⓭ toy department
⓮ men's department
⓯ information desk
⓰ cosmetics department
⓱ jewelry department

⓲ shoe department
⓳ food court
⓴ leather goods department
㉑ lockers
㉒ underground parking garage

7-1 Vehicles

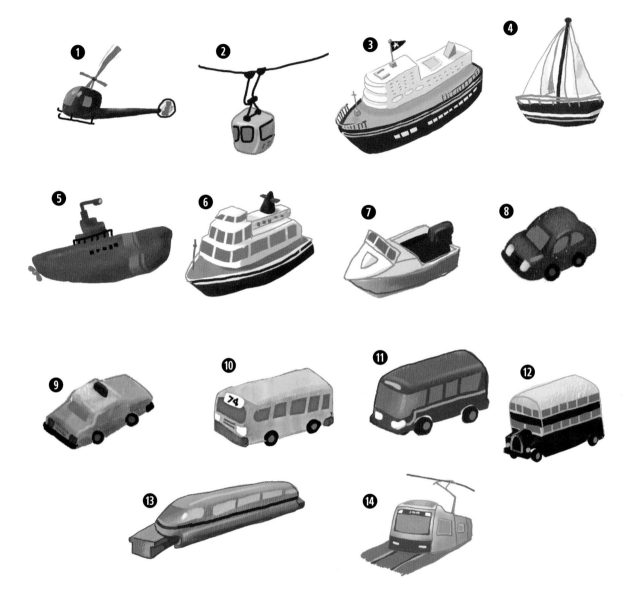

❶ helicopter
❷ cable car
❸ ocean liner
❹ sailboat
❺ submarine
❻ ferry
❼ motorboat

❽ car
❾ taxi
❿ bus
⓫ tour bus
⓬ double-decker bus
⓭ monorail
⓮ tram

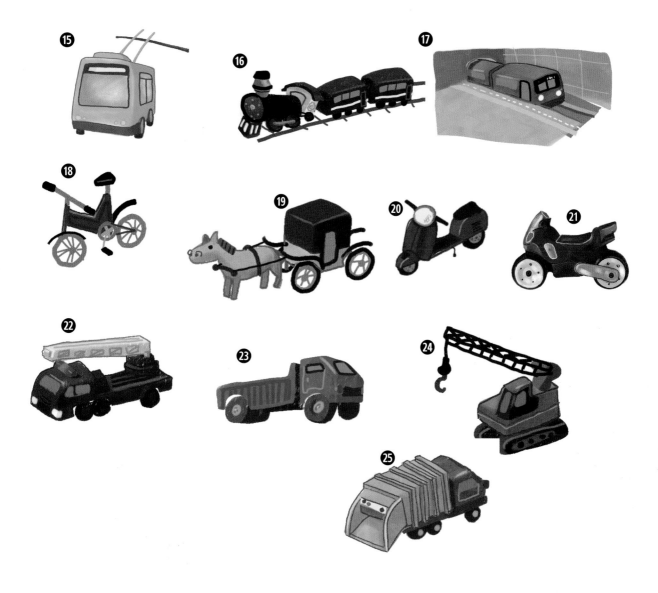

⓯ trolley bus

⓰ train

⓱ subway

⓲ bicycle

⓳ horse-drawn carriage

⓴ scooter

㉑ motorcycle

㉒ fire engine

㉓ truck

㉔ crane

㉕ garbage truck

❶ park

❷ pedestrian bridge

❸ corner

❹ street sign

❺ subway entrance

❻ road

❼ sidewalk

❽ bus stop

❾ gas station

❿ freeway

⓫ sports car

⓬ intersection

⓭ crosswalk

⓮ streetlight

⓯ traffic light

⓰ arcade

⓱ underpass

⓲ curb

⓳ parking space

❶ lavatory, toilet

❷ flight attendant

❸ emergency exit

❹ window blind

❺ tray

❻ seat pocket

❼ life preserver

❽ overhead compartment

❾ window seat

❿ aisle seat

⓫ seat belt

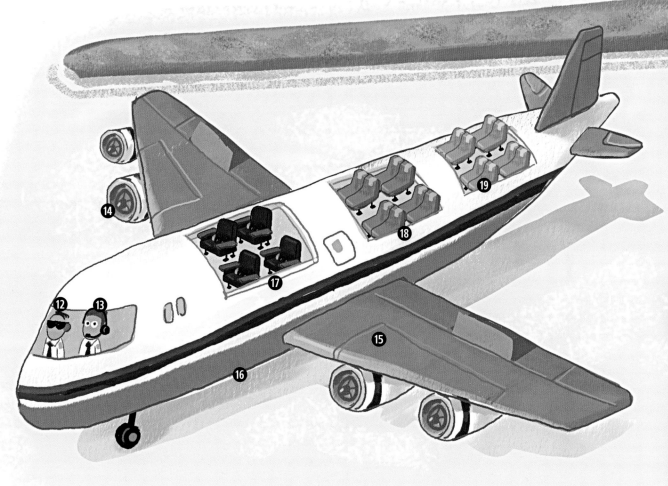

⑫ copilot

⑬ captain

⑭ jet engine

⑮ wing

⑯ fuselage

⑰ first class

⑱ business class

⑲ economy class

❶ terminal

❷ currency exchange

❸ insurance counter

❹ check-in counter

❺ landing

❻ airplane

❼ airline service counter

❽ passenger

❾ airline representative

❿ luggage

⓫ luggage cart

⓬ skycap

⓭ customs

⓮ immigration

⓯ luggage carousel

⓰ departure lobby

⓱ information desk

⓲ control tower

⓳ duty-free shop

⓴ duty-free item

㉑ shuttle bus

㉒ runway

㉓ takeoff

1 to play chess
2 to play Chinese checkers
3 to play cards
4 to play mahjong
5 to paint
6 to sculpt
7 to dance
8 hiking
9 mountain climbing
10 camping
11 to fish

⑫ gardening

⑬ to bird-watch

⑭ to sing

⑮ window shopping

⑯ to photograph

⑰ to read

⑱ to listen to music

⑲ to watch TV

⑳ to watch movies

㉑ to play video games

㉒ to surf the Internet

❶ saxophone

❷ flute

❸ clarinet

❹ oboe

❺ trombone

❻ French horn

❼ trumpet

❽ tuba

❾ harmonica

❿ guitar

⑪ bass guitar

⑫ harp

⑬ violin

⑭ cello

⑮ piano

⑯ electric keyboard

⑰ accordion

⑱ tambourine

⑲ drum

⑳ xylophone

❶ ambulance

❷ ward

❸ patient

❹ ear, nose, and throat doctor

❺ operating room

❻ ICU

❼ dentist

❽ pediatrician

❾ obstetrician

❿ ophthalmologist

⓫ internal medicine specialist

⓬ surgeon

⑬ nurses' station

⑭ nurse

⑮ crutch

⑯ walker

⑰ wheelchair

⑱ reception

⑲ patient information form

⑳ waiting room

㉑ stretcher

㉒ emergency room

❶ elementary school

❷ principal

❸ to get out from school

❹ kindergarten

❺ to attend school

❻ playground

❼ senior high school

❽ to get out from class

❾ public school

❿ private school

⓫ junior high school

⓬ to transfer to another school

⑬ alumnus

⑭ graduate school

⑮ institute of continuing education

⑯ bachelor's degree

⑰ master's degree

⑱ doctorate

⑲ dean

⑳ department chair

㉑ scholar

㉒ university

㉓ language class

㉔ to have class

❶ field

❷ track

❸ basketball court

❹ statue

❺ school gate

❻ bulletin board

❼ office

❽ principal's office

❾ classroom

❿ language lab

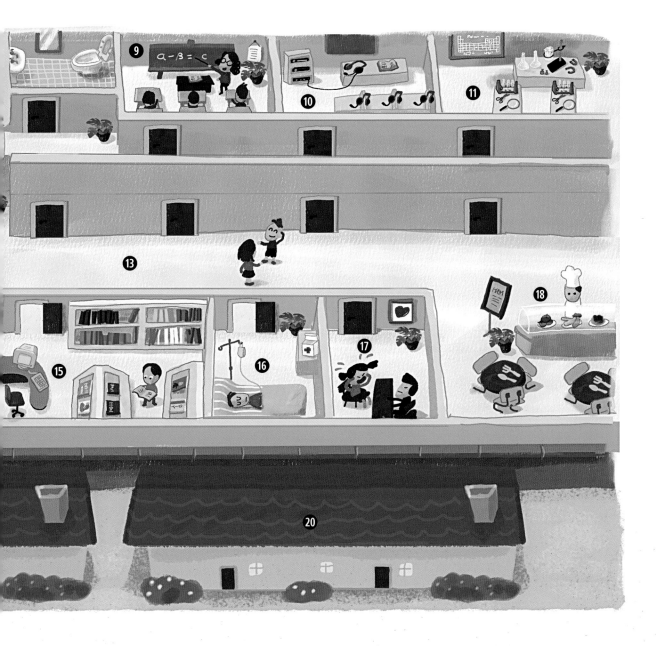

⓫ chemistry lab

⓬ lockers

⓭ hallway

⓮ auditorium

⓯ library

⓰ nurse's office

⓱ guidance counselor's office

⓲ cafeteria

⓳ gymnasium

⓴ dormitory

Part I   Courses

❶ subject	⑭ architecture
❷ French	⑮ geography
❸ Chinese	⑯ history
❹ English	⑰ astronomy
❺ Japanese	⑱ physics
❻ Spanish	⑲ chemistry
❼ foreign language	⑳ biology
❽ linguistics	㉑ medicine
❾ philosophy	㉒ law
❿ literature	㉓ political science
⑪ math	㉔ sociology
⑫ economics	㉕ music
⑬ engineering	㉖ physical education

Part II **Campus Life**

❶ semester

❷ homework

❸ essay

❹ exam

❺ monthly test

❻ midterm

❼ final exam

❽ oral presentation

❾ group discussion

❿ dictation

⓫ to cheat

⓬ to pass

⓭ to fail

⓮ scholarship

⓯ extracurricular activities

⓰ part-time job

⓱ to graduate

❶ chalkboard

❷ chalk

❸ eraser

❹ platform

❺ (pencil) eraser

❻ desk mat

❼ pencil case

❽ microphone

❾ book

❿ projector

⓫ textbook

⓬ chair

⓭ globe

⓮ map

⓯ book rack

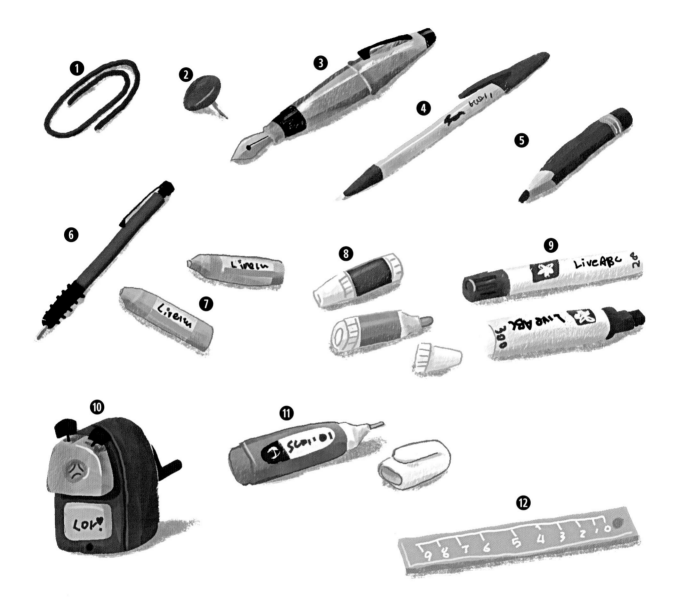

1. paper clip
2. thumbtack
3. fountain pen
4. ballpoint pen
5. pencil
6. mechanical pencil
7. crayon
8. color pen
9. marker
10. pencil sharpener
11. correction fluid
12. ruler

⑬ compass

⑭ stapler

⑮ scissors

⑯ glue

⑰ paint palette

⑱ paint

⑲ ink

⑳ notebook

㉑ sheet of paper

㉒ folder

1 red
2 pink
3 orange
4 yellow
5 green
6 blue
7 purple
8 brown
9 black
10 white
11 gray
12 beige
13 silver
14 gold
15 dark
16 light

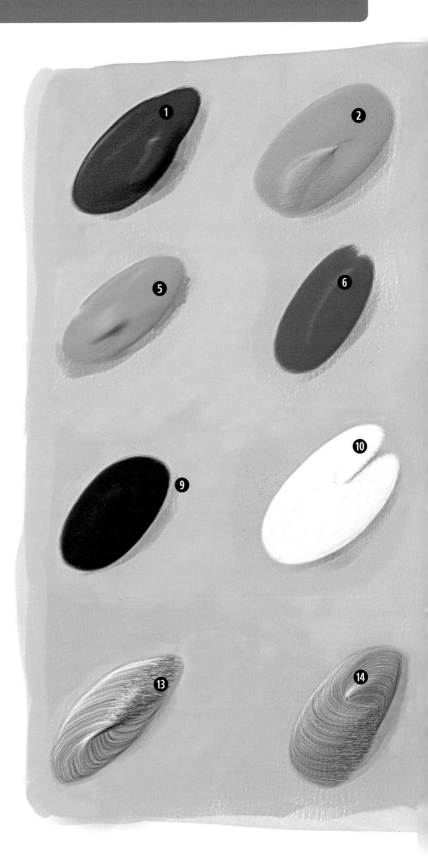

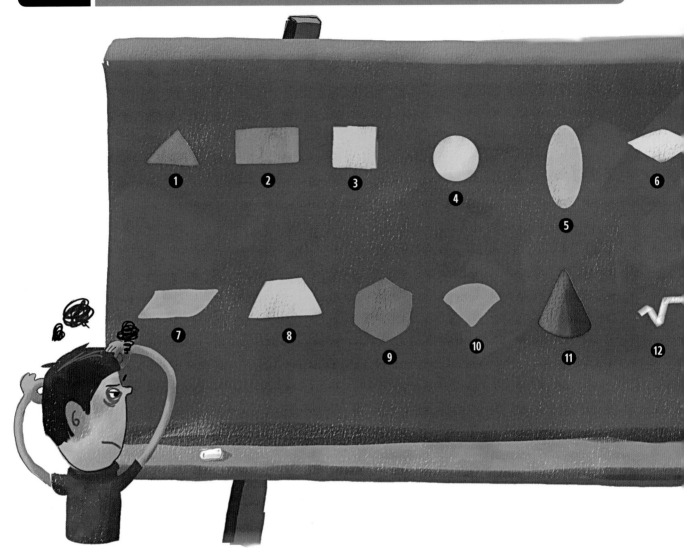

1. triangle
2. rectangle
3. square
4. circle
5. oval
6. diamond
7. parallelogram
8. trapezoid
9. polygon
10. sector
11. cone
12. square root symbol
13. plus
14. minus
15. multiplication
16. division
17. greater than
18. less than

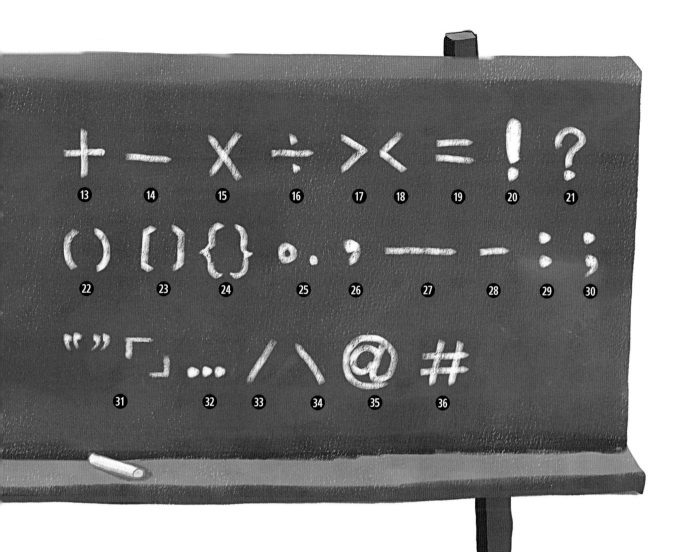

⑲ equal

⑳ exclamation point

㉑ question mark

㉒ parentheses

㉓ brackets

㉔ braces

㉕ period

㉖ comma

㉗ dash

㉘ hyphen

㉙ colon

㉚ semicolon

㉛ quotation marks

㉜ ellipsis

㉝ slash

㉞ backslash

㉟ "at" symbol

㊱ pound sign

❶ skydiving

❷ hang gliding

❸ boating

❹ white-water rafting

❺ swimming

❻ figure skating

❼ ice-skating

❽ roller skating

❾ speed skating

❿ archery

⑪ paintball
⑫ darts
⑬ jogging
⑭ cycling
⑮ horseback riding

⑯ car racing
⑰ skateboarding
⑱ snowboarding
⑲ skiing
⑳ rock climbing

❶ bowling

❷ basketball

❸ handball

❹ baseball

❺ dodgeball

❻ golf

❼ tennis

❽ softball

❾ table tennis

❿ ice hockey

⑪ field hockey

⑫ soccer

⑬ American football

⑭ billiards

⑮ volleyball

⑯ badminton

⑰ cricket

⑱ squash

⑲ bocce

❶ dog paddle

❷ breaststroke

❸ freestyle

❹ backstroke

❺ butterfly stroke

❻ sidestroke

❼ diving

❽ synchronized swimming

❾ waterskiing

❿ surfing

⓫ water polo

⓬ windsurfing

⓭ jet skiing

⓮ snorkeling

⓯ scuba diving

⓰ parasailing

1. hammer throw
2. discus throw
3. shot put
4. long jump
5. high jump
6. triple jump
7. hurdles
8. pole vault

❾ javelin throw

❿ steeplechase

⓫ marathon

⓬ relay race

⓭ sprint

⓮ racewalking

⓯ hundred-meter dash

❶ mouse	❾ monkey
❷ squirrel	❿ koala
❸ kangaroo	⑪ goat
❹ bat	⑫ sheep
❺ dog	⑬ cow, bull
❻ cat	⑭ horse
❼ rabbit	⑮ zebra
❽ pig	

⑯ camel

⑰ donkey

⑱ deer

⑲ giraffe

⑳ wolf

㉑ fox

㉒ rhinoceros

㉓ hippopotamus

㉔ panda

㉕ bear

㉖ lion

㉗ tiger

㉘ elephant

㉙ polar bear

1. fly
2. mosquito
3. bee
4. dragonfly
5. butterfly
6. moth
7. cicada
8. cockroach
9. cricket
10. spider
11. scarab beetle, June bug
12. ladybug
13. firefly
14. grasshopper

⑮ praying mantis

⑯ rhinoceros beetle

⑰ stag beetle

⑱ snail

⑲ ant

⑳ silkworm

㉑ earthworm

㉒ centipede

㉓ scorpion

㉔ flea

㉕ tadpole

㉖ frog

㉗ lizard

㉘ crocodile

㉙ snake

㉚ tortoise

❶ chicken

❷ turkey

❸ pheasant

❹ duck

❺ goose

❻ swan

❼ penguin

❽ seagull

❾ egret

❿ pigeon

⓫ sparrow

⓬ woodpecker

⓭ canary

⓮ crow

⓯ mynah

⑯ parrot

⑰ blue magpie

⑱ toucan

⑲ pelican

⑳ lark

㉑ hummingbird

㉒ swallow

㉓ shrike

㉔ owl

㉕ spoonbill

㉖ ostrich

㉗ peacock

㉘ eagle

㉙ vulture

㉚ condor

❶ crab

❷ lobster

❸ blowfish

❹ dolphin

❺ shark

❻ whale

❼ starfish

❽ sea cucumber

❾ sea snake

❿ sea horse

⓫ jellyfish

⓬ sea turtle

⓭ seal

⑭ mackerel

⑮ moray (eel)

⑯ sea bream

⑰ swordfish

⑱ clown fish

⑲ stingray

⑳ tropical fish

㉑ coral

㉒ seaweed

㉓ sea anemone

㉔ conch

㉕ flying fish

㉖ manatee

㉗ sea lion

❶ narcissus

❷ azalea

❸ lily

❹ daisy

❺ iris

❻ camellia

❼ rose

❽ cherry blossom

❾ carnation

❿ morning glory

⓫ lavender

⓬ sunflower

⑬ tulip

⑭ violet

⑮ canola

⑯ dandelion

⑰ shamrock

⑱ orchid

⑲ poinsettia

⑳ fern

㉑ willow

㉒ pine tree

㉓ cypress

㉔ maple

❶ January

❷ February

❸ March

❹ April

❺ May

❻ June

❼ July

❽ August

❾ September

❿ October

⓫ November

⓬ December

⓭ lunar calendar

⓮ year

⓯ month

⓰ day

⑰ date

⑱ Sunday

⑲ Monday

⑳ Tuesday

㉑ Wednesday

㉒ Thursday

㉓ Friday

㉔ Saturday

㉕ the day before yesterday

㉖ yesterday

㉗ today

㉘ tomorrow

㉙ the day after tomorrow

㉚ national holiday

㉛ time

㉜ hour

㉝ minute

㉞ second

❶ sun	❼ fog
❷ cloud	❽ frost
❸ rain	❾ snow
❹ wind	❿ ice
❺ thunder	⓫ hail
❻ lightning	⓬ storm

⓭ hurricane

⓮ tornado

⓯ low pressure

⓰ high pressure

⓱ cold front

⓲ cold current

⓳ temperature

⓴ spring

㉑ summer

㉒ fall, autumn

㉓ winter

㉔ sunny day

㉕ cloudy day

㉖ rainy day

❶ New Year

❷ New Year's Eve

❸ Valentine's Day

❹ Easter

❺ Halloween

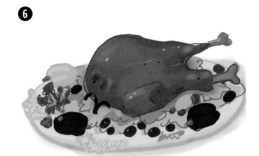

❻ Thanksgiving
❼ All Saints' Day
❽ Christmas
❾ Mother's Day
❿ Father's Day

131

   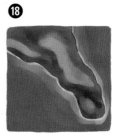 

❶ plateau

❷ forest

❸ lake

❹ waterfall

❺ river

❻ pond

❼ mountain

❽ valley

❾ basin

❿ plain

⓫ sandbar

⓬ beach

⓭ ocean, sea

⓮ island

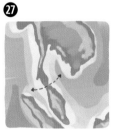 

⑮ strait
⑯ archipelago
⑰ coral reef
⑱ peninsula
⑲ bay
⑳ desert
㉑ dune

㉒ glacier
㉓ hills
㉔ bog, swamp
㉕ fjord
㉖ volcano
㉗ isthmus
㉘ rainforest

chest *35*

chest of drawers *17*

chicken *46, 120*

chicken breast *46*

chicken leg *46*

chicken nuggets *52*

chicken wing *46*

child *27*

children *29*

children's department *79*

chili sauce *63*

chin *35*

Chinese *98*

chop *61*

chopsticks *58*

Christmas *131*

cicada *118*

cinnamon *63*

circle *106*

civil servant *30*

clam *49*

clarinet *90*

classroom *96*

cleaning oil *15*

cleaver *20*

clock *4*

close *25*

clothespin *18*

cloud *128*

cloudy day *129*

clown fish *123*

coatrack *6*

cockroach *118*

cod *49*

coffee *50*

coffee shop *71*

coffeemaker *20*

coffeepot *54*

coin *76*

cola *50*

cold current *129*

cold front *129*

colon *107*

color pen *102*

comforter *17*

comma *107*

compact foundation *14*

compass *103*

conch *123*

conditioner *12*

condor *121*

cone *106*

control tower *87*

convenience store *70*

cook *24*

cooking oil *62*

copilot *85*

coral *123*

coral reef *133*

corn *44*

corner *83*

cornstarch *63*

correction fluid *102*

cosmetics *17*

cosmetics department *79*

cotton swab *13*

counter *20, 55, 76*

cousin *29*

cow *116*

CPU *8*

crab *122*

crack (an egg) *61*

crane *81*

crawl *38*

crayon *102*

cream *51*

cream puff *57*

credit card *77*

cricket *111, 118*

crocodile *119*

croissant *52*

crosswalk *83*

crow *120*

crutch *93*

cry *37*

cucumber *44*

cuff link *67*

cupboard *20*

curb *83*

currency exchange *76, 86*

curry *63*

curtain *4*

customer *40*

customs *87*

cut *61*

cutting board *20*

cycling *109*

cypress *125*

desktop computer *8*

dessert fork *58*

diamond *106*

dictation *99*

dinner knife *58*

discus throw *114*

dishrack *20*

dishwasher *20*

display counter *78*

diving *112*

division *106*

do a handstand *38*

do the laundry *24*

doctor *32*

doctorate *95*

dodgeball *110*

dog *116*

dog paddle *112*

doggie bag *52*

dolphin *122*

donkey *117*

door *4*

doorman *2*

dormitory *97*

double bed *17*

double-decker bus *80*

doughnuts *52*

down coat *65*

dragonfly *118*

drain *11*

dress *64*

drink *24*

drinking yogurt *51*

driver *30*

drum *91*

dryer *19*

duck *120*

dune *133*

dustpan *19*

duty-free item *87*

duty-free shop *87*

duvet *17*

DVD *9*

DVD player *7*

DVD-ROM drive *9*

E

eagle *121*

ear, nose, and throat doctor *92*

earrings *66*

earthworm *119*

Easter *130*

eat *24*

economics *98*

economy class *85*

eel *48*

eggplant *44*

egret *120*

elderly man *26*

elderly woman *26*

electric drill *22*

electric keyboard *91*

electric razor *12*

electric thermos pot *20*

elementary school *94*

elephant *117*

elevator *78*

ellipsis *107*

e-mail *73*

embarrassed *36*

emergency exit *84*

emergency room *93*

engineer *32*

engineering *98*

English *98*

entrepreneur *32*

envelope *72*

equal *106*

eraser *101*

escalator *78*

essay *99*

exam *99*

exchange rate *77*

excited *36*

exclamation point *106*

Index

ink *103*

institute of continuing education *95*

insurance counter *86*

internal medicine specialist *92*

intersection *83*

intestines *35*

iris *124*

iron *18*

iron the clothes *24*

ironing board *18*

island *132*

isthmus *133*

Index

saleswoman *30*

salmon *48*

salt *62*

salt shaker *55*

sandals *68*

sandbar *132*

sandwich *56*

sashimi *56*

Saturday *127*

saucer *59*

sausage *47*

saxophone *90*

scale *13*

scallop *49*

scanner *9, 40*

scarab beetle *118*

scarf *66*

scholar *95*

scholarship *99*

school gate *96*

scientist *32*

scissors *103*

scooter *81*

scorpion *119*

screw *22*

screwdriver *22*

scrub brush *23*

scuba diving *113*

sculpt *88*

sculptor *33*

sea *132*

sea anemone *123*

sea bream *123*

sea cucumber *122*

sea horse *122*

sea lion *123*

sea snake *122*

sea turtle *122*

seafood *40*

seagull *120*

seal *122*

seat belt *84*

seat pocket *84*

seaweed *123*

second *127*

secretary *30*

sector *106*

security camera *76*

security guard *76*

semester *99*

semicolon *107*

senior high school *94*

September *126*

serving tray *53*

sesame oil *62*

sew *24*

shampoo *12*

shamrock *125*

shark *122*

sheep *116*

sheet *17*

sheet of paper *103*

shelf *11*

shirt *64*

shish kebab *56*

shoe department *79*

shoes *68*

shopping bag *40*

shopping cart *40*

shorts *64*

shot put *114*

shovel *23*

shower cap *13*

shower curtain *11*

shower gel *12*

showerhead *11*

shrike *121*

shrimp *48*

shuttle bus *87*

shy *37*

sidestroke *112*

sidewalk *83*

signature *77*

silk scarf *66*

silkworm *119*

silver *104*

simmer *60*

sing *89*

singer *33*

single bed *17*

sink *11, 20*

sister *29*

sister-in-law *29*

sit *39*

skateboarding *109*

skiing *109*

skim milk *51*

skirt *64*

skycap *86*

skydiving *108*

slash *107*

sleep *24*

slice *61*

slip *38*

slippers *17, 69*

smile *37*

smoothie *50*

snail *119*

snake *119*

sneakers *68*

snorkeling *113*

snow *128*

snowboarding *109*

snowshoes *69*

soap *12*

soccer *111*

sociology *98*

socket *11*

socks *69*

soda *50*

sofa *4*

sofa bed *17*

softball *110*

soldier *30*

sole *49*

son *29*

son-in-law *29*

soup *56*

soup plate *59*

soy sauce *62*

spaghetti *57*

Spanish *98*

sparrow *120*

speaker *9*

speed skating *108*

spider *118*

spinach *45*

sponge *23*

spoon *58*

spoonbill *121*

sporting-goods department *78*

sports car *83*

sportswear *65*

spouse *29*

spring *129*

sprinkle *61*

sprint *115*

square *106*

square root symbol *106*

squash *111*

squat *38*

squid *49*

squirrel *116*

stag beetle *119*

stair *3*

stamp *72, 77*

stand *38*

stapler *103*

star fruit *43*

starfish *122*

statue *96*

steak *56*

steak knife *58*

steam *60*

steam cooker *20*

steeplechase *115*

stepdaughter *29*

stepson *29*

stereo *7*

stew *60*

stingray *123*

stir-fry *60*

stockings *69*

stomach *35*

stool *52*

storm *128*

strait *133*

straw *52*

strawberry *42*

street *70*

street sign *83*

streetlight *83*

stretch *39*

stretcher *93*

subject *98*

submarine *80*

subway *81*

subway entrance *83*

suit *64*

summer *129*

sun *128*

Sunday *127*

sunflower *124*

sunglasses *66*

sunny day *129*

sunscreen *14*

surfing *113*

surf the Internet *89*

surgeon *92*

surprised *36*

sushi *56*

swallow *121*

swamp *133*

swan *120*

sweater *65*

sweep the floor *24*

sweet potato *44*

swimming *108*

swimming pool *2*

switch *4*